learning to dance

Thomas Rain Crowe

Copyright © 2015 by Thomas Rain Crowe

All Rights Reserved

FIRST PRINTING

Fern Hill Books is an imprint of
New Native Press and amazon.com
books. www.newnativepress.org

Cover illustration/photo from amazon.com
Title page print by Hiroshige

ISBN:1-883197-46-5

Library of Congress Control Number: 2015912479

10 9 8 7 6 5 4 3 2 1

CONTENTS

LETTING LOVE FAIL   *9*

Letting Love Fail
Wind in a Galleon's Sails
Sometimes a Piece of Light
The Truth
The Test
After a Quarrel
Never is Not Enough
Love
The Personified Street
Oeillade
Cenotaph

LEARNING TO DANCE   *21*

Learning To Dance
Anathema
The Devil As Dervish
Pirouette
Winter
Where Are the Tears
Esplanade

LIVING ON MAIL   *29*

Living on Mail
Ways For Finding a Man
The Wish of a Spider Moon
When Stillness, My Body Like a Rock
How Can You Be So Near To Me
Vulnerability
The Shy Moon
Prisoners That Volunteer

How I Am Waiting

WHAT IS WOVEN   *41*

What Is Woven
Oh Love
Mirrors of the Moon
Why Does the Wind
The Dying
Love Poems From Persia

DEEP LANGUAGE   *49*

Deep Language
Under the Trees
First Light
Pieces. Of the Real Thing
The Lie That Lives
Seeing Through Stone
Sage

SHE WAS THE SEA   *59*

She Was the Sea
Black Like Soft Blue Wind
Meetings
Song for the Sometimes
Four For Beauty
Dolphins
The Nest
There Are No Snakes In Ireland
Voice
Making Love In the Lightning
Netherworlds
Not Even The Nil of Night
Say the Unspoken Word

IRIS   *75*

Iris
Mood Swings
The Garden
Translation
Breast Feeding
Wet Roads
Homelands
Writing
Poem For a Man Married To Mountains
Firsts
This Ink Is the Earth
Lei
The Lie That Lives
The Wild Ducks at Coole
The Florescent Eye
The Alma Mater of a Kiss
Immortality
Where the White Waves
The Blue Rose of Venice
Dancing in the Piazza San Marco
Last Love Poem

ACKNOWLEDGEMENTS   *98*

ABOUT THE AUTHOR   *99*

*Knowing nothing shuts the iron gates;
the new love opens them.
The sound of the gates opening,
wakes the beautiful woman asleep.
Kabir says: Fantastic!
Don't let a chance like this go by!*

The Perfect Work

Love is the perfect work.
A music which rings all the bells in the temple.
A special wind in the trees --

Listen to the way the drummer hits
lovingly his drum.
The way the dancer moves
over the warm earth.
And watch as children
leave their bodies behind on the old logs
around the fire and sing!

The world is aglow in the shadows of the
children singing. Of the sticks against
wood. Of the heavy silent breathing of the old ones
who sit off to the sides of the circle and pray.

When I am at work in my garden
I take off my shoes. I let
my other hands embrace dirt.
I plant myself in this place.
And knowing what love is, I
awake. In this place in my body.
Full of dream music.
Full of life.

I.

LETTING LOVE FAIL

LETTING LOVE FAIL

Somewhere, a man or a woman is waiting to love you.
Will your blindness ever reveal to you
any open door?

If pain has closed your eyes
to new things, then how are you going to see?

Come out of the cave!

Open the windows of your heart to this new spring.
The wind is out there too. Let it in.
It has a million poems for you
it wants to recite.
And thousands of kisses and dreams…

With your hands up over your ears,
your lover's voice
will pass you by like lost silences
dancing blindfolded in the night.

WIND IN A GALLEON'S SAILS

*"Most of what we do in life,
 even if we advance other reasons,
 is done because of women."*
           -Hermann Hesse

Let the words flow through me
like wind in a galleon's sails
And I will reach
to the nearest star
pluck a thousand smiles
she will receive as roses
in a miser's bouquet

For us the sun is taboo
We carry our hearts in cloth totebags
strapped to the middle of our lives

THE MUSE IS SINGING

The sky is dry and
there are lies in my moustache

She was clean
yet wanted to live near the floor
Her breasts were full of light
all men alone at night
read their whorey books by
Paris sang
Weeping to the echoes of lamantines

Pendant la Fete Noir
I am going to step out of this body
like wind in the sails of a galleon
She is the boom in my existence
The anchor in my joy

SOMETIMES A PIECE OF LIGHT

Sometimes a piece of light
is all of you remained.

I felt a strange heat in my chest
as if anger were building a fire.

We have passed the stage of being coy.
And the sun sets on opposite sides
of our same but different lives
into which we are pounding blue nails.

It was everything

and nothing in the same breath.
What mind is to memory.
What perfection is to pain.

Where were we born?
Does the snow still lie warm
on those places?
Where all that was written
now seems so much straw.
Where we made the vows of children
that touched our toy skin.

We were hiding in the throngs
that milled in the streets of big cities
in a dark night's sky.

We saw love in a carpenter's sheath.
Building skyscrapers from our dreams.

THE TRUTH

*"I cannot love a friend
whose love is words."*
        -Sophocles

The beginning was bliss.
Nothing came between us.
Not even time. Not even space.
We kept the same hours.
We ate the same foods.

IT MUST HAVE BEEN THE TRUTH

Other things began to catch her eye.
She found excuses for her beauty.
Compensation for her age.
She hid in books and silence.
And in the bodies of her children.

Her love each night
was brought to me in blocks of dry ice.
We lived alone in the same rooms.

Soon we lived alone.
We met at theatres and cafes.
Or by mistake in the park.

Our old home seemed empty.
I passed by on the city bus.
Heavy bolts guarded her inside.
She loved me. There were other men.

She loved us all.
We had nothing.

THE TEST

In her mind she has tested God.
I could see it in her eyes,
like rusted rings around the moon.
If art were for hire
we'd all be dressed in business suits
and carry a deadly weapon on each hip.
I wouldn't call this a conspiracy,
just something weird that's happening
in all our beds on boring nights.

She knows three things that excite her.
I wipe the love from typewriter keys.

Franz Liszt.
Sex in the back seat of Chevrolets.
The sea.

AFTER A QUARREL

I know good sex will melt
the stars
And good wine
dazzles the sky
But who am I to
cuddle with angels
or drink champagne from a rich man's ear
Deep in the embrace of reason
sparks flicker to the touch of candles
Whispers shout
blind as bone
And we cover each other with our bleeding hair

NEVER IS NOT ENOUGH

Only Armageddon
could have planted a garden like this.
Nightshade amongst the flowers.
And horsethistle hiding in the beans.
Even *ali-ali-in-free* won't bring this heart
of mine back home.
Near the fire-warmth
of what our life might be.

Here, the green hell in these hills
is turning blue.
Almost black with each day that
looks more and more like night.
Where I search for you in sheets
or in shadows waiting to be born.

Never is not enough.
Not when we have knocked on heaven's door.
And been to breakfast with God
eating quarks and bacon, eternity and eggs…

Never is not enough.
I see you in every ant.
In every lily that breaks free from the grass.
In every line that brings meaning to the poem.
Like the death of fire
dowsed by a typhoon of tears.
Drowning the years.

I was once an artist, now a clown.
Ashes, ashes, all fall down…

LOVE

While looking at the beauty in a rose,
I fell in love.
In love with the flower,
not the face of the girls of my dreams.
Now, I sit all day and night
beside this red rose and weep.
So much beauty it gives to my eyes.
So sweet its red perfume.

I have grown old sitting her all
night and day. Years and generations
have gone by.
Women have passed by
and asked for my hand.
But I just kept staring and fondling this rose.

Now, I'm not sure whether it is me
or the rose that wants to die.
Its petals, one by one,
are falling to the ground.
My ears are bad and I can barely see.

There is nothing sadder than
the death of the body or
the end of love.
When I leave this world I
will never come back.
Unless it is to come back as a lover
or a rose.

THE PERSONIFIED STREET

"At night, the self only desires
to steep its clangor in softness,
in woman..."
        -Vladimir Mayakovsky

If the truth be known
every mountain is a hill.
Every blade of grass a tree.
Is this confusing size with sex?
Or only something like rain with snow.
Let's pretend there's a meadow in your dream
and we're both trains.
Who will finish first?
Engine or caboose?

Peace is like a parade
through the heart of New York.
Sex is the street.
I am the fifty-second floor of mankind
that covers you in a confetti of lovenotes
falling like martyrs from my eyes…
You are looking up and saying "yes" with
your thighs wide at the crossroad.

Brass bands passing into the womb.

OEILLADE

She said it with her eyes.
With lashes and lids in a single glance.
It was her six o'clock silence
that cut through doors and
windows that somehow took leave of my heart.
"Never marry a man who won't dance,"
she said, aiming a camera
at me like a hot poker, then
taking pictures of the noise.

There was nothing in me that she didn't like,
yet her passion perceived me as an empty room.
A lounge without chairs. An antechamber
without a wall of mirrors.

Whenever I opened my mouth,
apartheid fell out on the floor.
Prisoners of war or
the colors of fresh-cut grass—
It was the green she loved.
It had to be. There was nothing left
in the house to hock but air
coming in between boards in the wall
on a windy day.
"Love is this," she said.
"Like something sucking at our veins."

Today there is sunshine,
then it rains.
The damn pursing of lips.
Feet that can't move to simple melody.
The screaming of her eyes.

CENOTAPH

You touch me,
but I am not here.
I am out shopping or
in another century if I am to believe
the words coming from your hands.
When I turn to touch you back
you are there, but busy building walls
and my fingers caress cold rock
of an empty tomb.

II.

LEARNING TO DANCE

LEARNING TO DANCE

for Nanna

I am disappearing
into the side of her body.
Her body, which when it lifts
and turns, also moves the Earth.
I have given up the toys
of my childhood
and my ambitions for old age.
And have moved deep within
the walls of her silver skin.

I am through with my love of suffering.
And the words that describe that love.
I am going to carry on a magnificent
affair with the wind
        from the inside of her body
        where we both sleep.

Friends, I am going deeper, even
        deeper inside than the animal
        or a blade of grass—
I am looking for the stones.
The stones that lay to the side
and in the bed of The Great River.
Among those stones
there is only one rock with my name.
I will pick it up
and hold it high above my head
in the inner light.

I will know many things.

Outside, with her body, she
is teaching the world to dance!

ANATHEMA

A long hush had fallen over the great city.
Everything stood.
Still.
On a country road
a solitary rider
rode through night.
Unaware.
It was time for change.
A heavy tear
rolled through the streets.

He slept in a small room
on a floormat.
Kept doves
for luck in a cage.
Her hair silver
like shadows of the moon,
stood out
against the darkness in his dreams.
She saw he had kind hands.
And a strong heart.
She was a dancer
and dined with elegance and grace.
He worked in wood.
Ate food grown on his own land.

They had the same eyes.
They sang different songs.

THE DEVIL AS DERVISH

Here is the wisdom that weeps.
And the crying that
crushes stone:

I'M ALL HEART!

And even the buildings blush.
The trees turn black.
Or the cities
sing "Blue-Eyed Girl."

I felt the 10,000 things
in her thighs.
The Path and The Way
in the way she danced.

And in the distance of whose eyes
do you think she is trying to be?
Just a mirage—

So let the drums
and the dance begin.
As I dervish this devil inside
into sleep.
Where he belongs.
Alone.
Where she sang.
As the spring birds danced
in the memory of darkened glass
in the mirrors of her eyes.

PIROUETTE

To describe the way you dance
would be like giving names
again to all the trees.
Or selling land
back to wolf and bear.

The white rocks
here beside a dry summer's stream
are living on heat.
And water from melted snow
is quenching their stolen thirst.

In six days
you danced through every foot of my life.
Moving doors and windows
until there was nowhere to get in.
I watched and said nothing.
And, like the last spin of a pirouette,
watched you turn
and go…

WINTER

What could be colder than a winter with you not there,
I don't know.

Maybe ice in the corner of a spring dream.
Maybe words in the field of a draught.

Somewhere they are building a city
where all our country dreams will come true.
Where art walks with daylight arm-in-arm
down streets of nothing to lose.

So they won't let you dance in the nude.
And you come each year at Christmas
in your green Chinese coat to the park
to say goodbye.
To watch the old men swat pigeons with their canes.

Maybe the answer is an old house in the country to the north.
Your stage dress covered in glass.
My thoughts on something to think.
Or a new name.

It's all there.
Somewhere where your feet have still missed pain.
In the corner of a dream.
Or the absence of shame—

Or wherever I am standing on the side of a ship at sea
and your eyes are my memory of land.

WHERE ARE THE TEARS

Where are the tears I would cry
if indeed you flew away?
They are hidden
deep in a sea of need.
Beyond the closets of all time.

You made marks in the sand
with the way you tried to fly.
And the velvet scars on my eyes
from your smile
are the only things that see.

To write "I'm gone"
on the end of my life is not enough.
Nor to picture pirates on the sea—
I am the weighmaster
of many years to come.
You have put your love
to the scales.
And there was equal weight.
On both sides your dreams could dance!

You are almost the sky
when the land now is almost dead.
A thousand prayers.
The sound of a pony's hooves
echoing against the midnight sand.

ESPLANADE*
> *"To praise is the whole thing."*
> *-R.M. Rilke*

There's an Orphic moon
in our eyes that is calling out "love."
And between sugar and God
there is a choice I must make to be free.
Like graveyards living
in the parks of New York.
Or business buildings
in the meadows of peace.

To build a house one must
first build a bottom floor.
To worry about walls, or
wonder if the roof will leak
means the floor is not strong.

Finish, perfectly, that floor.
Then, go on to other things.

I am looking for the source.
The source of all that is Real.
So if you are looking for
holes in the middle of night
or poems that never bleed,
then get used to the echoes of walls
and life as lazy as
the love you hang on dying trees
to dry.

To feel is the whole thing.

For a blind man rarely sees.
Ah yes, there is new power
in the eyes of these hands!

*an open stretch of grassy ground
 designed for walking along the shore.

III.

LIVING ON MAIL

LIVING ON MAIL

It's not only hope,
it's the letters have kept me alive
all these years.
My mailbox
like a big black belly,
always hungry,
always dying of thirst.
Rumbling and grumbling for
only the best of food.

Sometimes, during periods of drought,
there is not enough ink or love in the world
to go around.
My mailbox shrinks.
My body weakens.
And a time of darkness comes.

But bad times,
like my old friend says,
are the same as good times.
Neither lasts.

So I pick up thick books.
Take long walks.
And think of her all day—
Until the groans from my middle
and my mailbox cease.
And there is mail.
And a flicker's unchained laugh
echoing wildly through the woods!

WAYS FOR FINDING A MAN

For three days
the women neither eat nor sleep
In ancient passage
as they sit in prayer and song
musing on the promise of a man

In Kathmandu, breads and sweets
purify the air seducing the young noses of men
waiting in line
Parlor incense lounging in the pillows
that will welcome, later, their sex-filled sleep
Fiddle and drum resounding from the woods…

THE WISH OF A SPIDER MOON

Here, the moonlight
is weaving silver threads of peace around
every darkened heart.

I walk alone through the elderberry
in silence
singing back to the birds
their songs

and wishing she were here.

WHEN STILLNESS, MY BODY LIKE A ROCK

When stillness, my body like a rock
can move nothing, nothing moves.
Nothing even from this earth
I use as a bed.
Not a single word upon
an empty piece of white.
Not even pain.

Every star in the sky
is a hole that somehow leads to you.
And I, ladderless,
am here to stand reaching
from this unladdered land.

Yesterday
the rain showed me your face
in every silver tear.
In every green leaf I felt
the soft spring grace of your skin.

And memory returned!

Yes, there's still a great weight
in the fear I drink each day
alone in this darkness.
And I know its kind of heat
that can heal. Yet,
when stillness, my body like a rock
can move nothing,

nothing moves.

HOW CAN YOU BE SO NEAR TO ME

How can you be so near to me
when your feet dangle in that ocean
and this ocean plays with mine?

If it isn't the water that joins
then all that's left is air.
That carries your love
to me in a gust of wind
each day.
As if your fingers ran
through my lovesick hair.
And a moment's peace
like the yawn of the moon,
settled down by my side
here on this mountain
with the wind
and the dew.

VULNERABILITY

I built labyrinths around my world
in glass.
Walls of brick and stone.
Hard earth floors.
And a roof that would never leak.

In the one space that I left
between the stones
for the world outside to somehow speak to mine,
I built a window
of the lightest and densest air.

The world inside those red and gray walls
stood as still as the space between words.
And though there were no doors,
somehow she got in.
And the dark and silent safeness of those rooms
turned to villages of light!

But her wings began to wither
and die.
Like the wild flowers of fall.
Set into jars
for the tables of imprisoned life.
Weaned from their own roots.

I tore at the perfect roof!
Broke out the walls of brick and stone!
Shattered all the glass!

As she flew out
toward the sun in her own sky,
I felt her entering my body.
Going deeper and deeper inside as she danced.
And there,
standing on a floor of solid earth,
I became different.

And I was near the ocean.
Like a stallion of light
running free across the seashore sand.

THE SHY MOON

What she knows
she wears on her cuffs like lace.
Hides
in her furrows and frowns
like a dream.
Watching women
through windows of night
like a city madam
in a suburb of peeping-toms.

What deceptive and distant arc
is she making?
What mischief now
does she plan in those barndoor eyes?

Here on Earth,
the moonlight is weaving webs around every darkened heart.
And you'd think this small green bottle of death
would bring new wine to an old life.
But it can't.
There is too much of her
still hidden in my eyes.
And it's all that I can see.

PRISONERS THAT VOLUNTEER

At three in the morning
locked away I thought, safely,
from the demons of any town,
she broke into my home
with a gun
and a threatening look
drug me out
into the back of a foreign blue car.

She tied me up in scarves to
the bedposts. Guatemala
stuffed in my mouth
for several weeks
tortured me
with affection,
artichokes,
lies,
French poetry, soufflés,
sensual massage, and the threat
of never going to let me go.

After months of being lashed
with brown eyes
and a special country love,
she one day took off
the binds.
Opened the door of the cage.

I stood at the door of her small country house
looking out at the redwoods.

Picked up the scarves from the floor.

Gave her both my wrists.

HOW I AM WAITING

In Nature
there is nothing with names,
only one big body to protect from
the best intentions of men.

I see in her eyes the need
to touch again the trees.
To know a man again
for the first time.

How far away from the tips
of each other's hands we are.
So many miles.
Yet, the moon as it glistens
on the surface of a small mountain pond nearby
has given me the strength.
The trust.

And I wait.

IV.

WHAT IS WOVEN

WHAT IS WOVEN
for Karen

It's like the way the wood is thread
into the arms of the loom that I love you.
How each strand of silk is a step
in the dance of the way you weave
has me married to this dream of cloth.

What is brought together in embrace
is woven.
The bond of warmth in winter's bed.
Or the white
lightly flowing in the hair of a bride.

The parts of the whole in a piece of cloth
are the strings that come to me as kisses.
A million lips that have sculpted my face.
And in black and white I am the gift of the rug
that lies in reverence at your feet.

With the rhythm of the silent song the loom sings,
I am learning to talk to the moon.
To the sun and stars.
And to the trees the secret words of the dance…
Oh love, what pattern are we weaving with
the back and forth of this dance?
Not until this spinning wheel of yarn
has run out will we know the form
that together we will take:
the *weft* of one body that's free.

That which is completed together
is woven.
Woven as the wood in a window to glass.
And the way that my heart is sewn to your door
I will love you:
a piece of morning
sleyn and embroidered on the *reed* of night!

OH LOVE

Oh love
Where do you go with your silence?
I am moving into
the infinite walls of your skin
in search of our being.
Only this oneness knows
eternity's secret to prayer.
Or the music of spheres
which I have seen whirling in your eyes.

From a sacred rock
together we saw the ancient dance of stone.
How the mist reveals the mountains
and the mountains move!

Somewhere through the non-existent doors of my heart,
an eagle will fly,
and this race of wind in my mind
will cease.
And there again we will meet.
God looking God in the eye
on the firsts full moon of fall.

You have come to me
like the very first beat of my heart.
The first breath.
Or happiness
showing itself in tears
or smiles that will forever glow.

Oh love,
as I move deep into the gardens of your dreams,
you are still asleep in me.
Every miracle that a man with a woman can be.
You are everything.
Sight. Sound. Touch.
And the Ancient One

walking in silence from the sea…
You are everything.
The silence.
The song.
And the one inside that is me.

MIRRORS OF THE MOON

I have seen my face in the moon.
It is the face of a man.
His eyes are like mirrors.
Looking into that glass
I am beautiful.
Now I have seen this beauty.
And my eyes sang like broken shells!
If I close my eyes,
will the man-in-the-moon go away?
I am tired of living only in the shadow of the sun!
In the aftershocks and echoes of my heart's desire.
If this were winter, I'd be dying of heat!

Oh love, where do you go with your silence?
This silence in the words we share is like food.
Fresh fruit. Or water from the deepest well.
Why must we cry when we are already wet?
And I lie near you
like a wounded angel breathing beauty from a bowl.

Oh love, how could we have come all this way
only to die?
Are you listening?
Even now, night is waiting in the mirrors of memory
for the last dance.
Where someday, our kisses will begin turning, again, to sleep.
And sleep   into the River of Dreams.

Open eyes!
Open, weary heart!
I am coming out of this music of sunrise, to dance!
I have seen my face in the moon.
It is your face.
Your eyes are like mirrors.
And I want you
even more than I want these words.

WHY DOES THE WIND

Why does the wind
keep calling out to me
your name?
The way I am away from the sea
yet the waves keep sliding in
to the shore.
The tight fit
of old hands sliding into a new glove.
Like the sudden spark of the match
that is prophecy of heat.
Or the way one bird dies
and two new are in that moment
born.

Oh love, as I leave this place
how my yearning grows!
Your face pouring through the
winter window glass as sun.
And as I say goodbye to the
sounds of heat we've made here for
only one day, I have already returned
with just the thought of you.
To a heart always burning here.
Inside.

THE DYING

The dying is in the dust.
How the old house covers the shelves
with its age. And the body
starts dreaming of sleep.

Under all this sleepless skin
there is another who is waiting to dance.
A heart
that sings love songs to snow.
And this part of a man
wrestling with the wit of God.

Oh love, are you listening?
To the groaning of good land.
To the thunder without rain.
To the pride of pleasure,
to the pain.

Meanwhile, night is waiting in the mirrors of memory
for the last dance.
Like being born is the blasphemy of light.
And someday our kisses will begin turning again
to sleep.
The fruit suddenly in love with the wine.
A table, growing old, that has found reverence for the trees.
And the gold that was once our bodies
now dancing in the ancient ashes of
an old house.
A memory
on this ancient land.

LOVE POEM FROM PERSIA
WHILE DRINKING BAD WINE

Oh love, look into this glass of wine.
Dark flowers circle in honey that
float in the dance of pure joy.

Drink the sweet blood that makes this man drunk
from kisses seeping from wet flame.

Here, hunger haunts fever in bone where
I am prisoner and soak up sugar like light
from the smoke you touch as my face.

No one knows why we growl as we sing this song.
Listen! The word which comes from the rose is "fire."

V.

DEEP LANGUAGE

DEEP LANGUAGE
for B.A.C.H.

Do the waves from the arms of the sea
Reach up from water
Into your body of perfect clay?

In the enthusiastic air
The wind sings its last summer song of salt
To the sleeping sand.
And this body
Walks the edge
Of water where it mates with earth.

I am here.
Planting seeds
On the beaches of things we would not believe.
Where this sea is kith
For painters who look into the eyes of this night.
Kin
For poets learning to pray.

In the morning
The dolphins and I will dance
And the man who is wild in me
Will come up from the water
Like the woman in you
Stands up in the earth.

Maybe it is the little bit of God in me
That is also you is teaching us
This dance.
The ebb and flow of the tide
That is singing this song
To the drums of the moon.

As the waves of evening
Pull up like blankets on the shoreline bed of sand,
The child in me is ready for sleep.

And wherever you are tonight
We are kith   and a kind of kin.
The way that shells whisper secrets
Or midnight sings
To the goddess of rock
The sound of these ancient words.

UNDER THE TREES

I am the
Lover who sings in the shadows
Of your garden dream. The man who
Vows to be faithful to a kiss.
Every woman who is listening knows
Your song. The way the wind blows through the roses
Of our sleep. While the god within us dances
Under the trees.

FIRST LIGHT

"By looking far out into space, we are also looking far back into time, back toward the horizon of the Universe, back toward the epoch of the Big Bang.
                    -Carl Sagan

Here in mountains
or in pastureland of stars
the fires of genesis dance
in the galaxies of a single stone.
In an atom that was once a sun.
And was burning in the first perfect moment of heat.

How can something simple as love
be measured by eons of expanding light?
A wisp of wind become breath for the sea?

Only in the darkness of ancient evening did she dance
in firelight to the music of his eyes.
Like a billion years without skin
that suddenly in an instant became body burst into flames!

How it must have been the first time
the sea made love to the thought of rain!
The first time God   entered space—
And the woman in water gave birth
to the seed of corn,   to sacred leaf...

Even in the evening she dreams of morning
in her sleep. Of that quiet moment before love
when creation paused
at the thought of dawn flooding his face.
When hands become legs and
bodies become the moving waves of sheets
covering the darkness before the birth of stars.
Before even the breath of Truth
became flames dancing from the dream
on fire in a poet's heart
and there was light!

53

PIECES. OF THE REAL THING

*"I was not yet in love, but I was in love
With love itself; and I sought for something
To love, since I loved loving."*
  -St. Augustine

I am liquid next to
your love
because I am not your love.
Love next to your body
because I am not yet whole.
Whole next to
your pieces
because I am not your eyes.
Eyes next to your heartbeat
because I am not your flame.
Child next to your flame
because I am not your fire.
Fire next to
the way you leave me
alive with my sadness,
because I am not your sadness.
One next to your quiet love,
because I am not Love.

Because I am only

pieces
of every part
of what is only
the only
real
thing.
And it's the way you make me
shy,
silent,
strong
that makes my silhouette white against

all this darkening land.
And so,
I am colors next to
your darkness.
Halos
next to your light.
Kisses
next to your kissing.
Because I am not you kissing.
And at night
how our sleeping body shines!

THE LIE THAT LIVES

Moments are only small eternities covered
In the silent centuries of your grace.
Cannons going off in the gunneries of
Another autumn day like a memory
   medicine men have conjured with love.

January has gone on long enough and
Eternity is weeping at night with
All the pain that distance brings when you're gone, and
Nothing will change the death of this little lie that
   is you in me
     that lives!

SEEING THROUGH STONE

"Where are you, my happiness?
Sorrow, gloom, confusion.
In the fields? Or in the pub?
Nothing but illusion..."
      -Sergei Esenin

No silhouette of your smile
will ever reach the ears of distant space.
All that will get there is dreams.
A million moonbeams glittering
in the stone from which wizards must have sculpted
your face.

After the sun goes down each day
there are a few seconds that no one sees.
A moment of darkness
before the sky, again, decides against night.

I wonder where we are
in that place that no one sees.
Wandering near heaven's trees.
Like children.
Lost in a wondrous woods.
Calling each other's name...

SAGE

He moves toward the west
from eastern hills calling her name.
From rich brown earth
to sand.
To golden beaches of love where only love
could find him under this moon.

She knows he is coming.
She knows it by the way the birds
whistle in air. The way
first spring leaves dance in sunlight
and heat rises like the invisible heartbeat in waves…

In the inlet tide-pool
they search water and sand for the
traces of prophecy in shells.
For those tiny scrolls
that tell the social history of tides.
The sexual biograph of moon.
The way water makes love to poetry
in the form of fragile stone—

In his search for sunlight he has found the sky.
Has found an ancient blueness in her body
of perfect clay.
In shallow water.
Where she kneels in the ebb and flow of language
digging for answers.
Digging for shells.
Lost in the runic wisdom of these waves.

VI.

SHE WAS THE SEA

SHE WAS THE SEA

She was the sea.
She was the sea shore.
She was the space between sand and the shoeless waves.
She wore the soles of her feet   like sandals
against the shard--like shells.
She sat at sunrise and
gave birth to the sun
coming up between her legs.
She was the sea.
She was what every seaman saw in foam.
What every seaman said he saw just beneath the water and
calling his name.
She was the siren manatee sage of liquid sky.
She not only swam but sailed like sailfish and squid
from the blind dark deep to the sex in an eye.
She was the sea.
She was scenery, never seen, looking back into
the artist's eyes.
Looking out beyond horizons to where infinity grows up
from the sky blue of nothing.
Where she is the sea.
Is the shy rage of sandollars sick of the rich.
Sick of the syringe-sick beach washing up
under the feet where she was.
She was the sea.
She was the c in the cartography of quenched desire.
Was the t in truth. Or the b
in the bottom sand sharking for the fire in lunch.
She was the smooth silk skin of a somnambulist dusk
doing DNA-things to the adolescent night.
Doing dangerous damage to my silent sleep where
only water was and now there are waves.
Waves where she was. Like the laser in light
laughing down on the seal-rock silly with seals.
Sober as sex. Wading in foot-foam
and the footprints of water where she was and
I am still walking. Here. Where. She was the sea.

BLACK LIKE SOFT BLUE WIND

Black like soft blue wind
that falls to the shoulders of the sea
is her hair,
is the siren sound of
how her smile only slightly shows
the silent sunburst of her face,
face following the line of destiny
from draught in to what water is
or was
had it been wedded to rock,
sound that as she speaks   sings!
Songs of ravensbreath mornings
searching the first glimpse of sun
for the sky.
Black like soft blue wind
I am in this song of watching
God grow from woman, goddess turn to roses
from sighs.
O moment of memory now only two days from distance,
let beauty make love these eyes!

MEETINGS (What If Words or We)

What if words or we were
star-crossed and afraid of the night.
Night lit with the way the moon mirrors
the caress of inner speech. Or
how the crossroads make love to
the echo of reflected light.
Wouldn't the wonder of winter
freeze if by chance our bodies should meet?
Should speak and become then-again ice.
Only the *escra* or
the excelsior of this thought can dance,
can do can-can on the grave of Death and
not die.
Here Hiroshima is
blowing kisses to the wind. To
the marriage of how next we will meet:
like two eyes searching for
what the lost in the other has said.
One the bleeder
and the other the one that has bled.
One the moonlight and
the other at the foot of the bed.

SONG FOR THE SOMETIMES

Somewhere in the silver web of moonlight,
your hair, I am weaving this song.
Song of the way the nape of your neck becomes
cradle for my lullaby of thoughts newborn and
fresh from the soil. Song of how
supple and firm is the hidden skin
connecting hip with toes and
how it wants to dance. Song with
more sounds than even the sound of breathing
has made me die—die to the deadsounds
of denying what never was love and
what lies. Song to the white-ivory innocence of
Handel-hands chording and caressing my flesh
like Mozart or music of the spheres. Song singing to
the impresario's whim of rain watering eyes and
eyelid at the web-spun crimson twilight end of day.
Song to the brook-born firefly lost in your knees that
makes me laugh and laugh loud at the way we
bob and weave, roll like rivers, around on and
away from this bed. Song for the sometimes
we meet in the timeless lock of lust embracing the night and
the thought of making love maybe one more time to
the first daylight dream of dawn. Song of this
sad song that can't sing to the pain of
going separate into that good night. That test of
tomorrow's shadowy greed that
takes you away from the mirrored blooming iris of these eyes.
Yet,
somewhere in the silver web of moonlight, your hair,
I am weaving this song.
Song disheveling the spider-like warp and
weft of the web from an overdose of dew or
the drug of choice tying my heart in wrongknots
that like this gentle addiction to the liquid
weave of you wrapping these bones
is home.

FOUR FOR BEAUTY

*"Enjoyment and not abstinence
is the food of intellect."*
           -William Blake

B etter than the best blue bird that
E ver flew from out of the ears of God
A nd disappeared into the blinding sun
U nder the moon that came up at
T he same time that I imagined I kissed
Y ou and instead of dreaming opened my eyes to
    See you there.

B ecause there is something more beautiful than
E ven the thought of you,
A nd that beauty sometimes speaks when I am
U p in the trees
T oo high to hear its voice yet knowing it is
Y ou.

B efore I was born I dreamed of a girl with
E yes that sang things so blue they
A lmost danced. When I saw you
U nder your clothes and I was a man,
T he skin on your bones jumped up like light-
Y ears to cover my sleep.

B y the time time took
E very look in your eyes
A way and I was left alone with only your name
U nder my breath, something told me
T o say your name again and when I did
Y ou took it back into your mouth from my lips
    and were mine.

DOLPHINS

I.

Down at the edge of twilight twisting and dancing
Over the mist in perfect waves we
Long to become what we are in the aren't of
People in the form of fins whistling our names and
How we reach out to touch the silky wetness of skin
In this dream of talking without words or even
Noise that has somehow become the sound of ocean
Somewhere where there is no water and I am lost in your eyes.

II.

Do we ever really do the right thing when
Our eyes meet and
Lips want to be hands if only to feel
Past the feeling of being touched, toyed with, tickled
Here where only a heart beats
In the middle of me learning to swim out beyond the
Nowhere of waves making light of the undertow knocking about
in my brain
So loud that deafness almost sounds like a kiss.

III.

Dawn moves like an arson into the end of night with
Our bodies bent like bullets moving through the shattered
reflection of glass
Long legs jealous of arms intertwined in a dance that can only be
Part of what an ocean wears to bed with
Half a moon for light lighting your face
In ways that only a man in love with himself can see
Not as something water would wrestle away from the dead like
Soft pearls stealing innocence from these fingers robbed of your
smile.

IV.

(Let's) Do what the dolphins do and dance
Out where the waves are nothing but a
Lovesong's tears wearing away the sand the way
Pirates take beauty away from its toys and
Hold it for ransom the way I would hold you
In my seasick arms if only we were two ships
Nearing the edge of night where only the eyes of dolphin shed
light on
Something as bright as a dream.

THE NEST
> *for N.*

When the men and their saws
brought the big tree down
>> and
the rough brown limbs had
been drug from the yard
>> and
the pain in the side of my heart
had shrunk from its swollen size
>> and
I could see the sky again,
there was a twig at my feet
that forked at the thin end
>> and
bridged by the beauty of a perfect nest.
A nest that I took back to
the house to look at
>> and
when I did, saw it was made from moss
>> and
grass, straw, twine, mud
>> and
something that shined like it held it
all together running around the in
>> and
out side of the nest at the top
>> and
at the bottom where a bird would sit
>> and
when I looked to find out what it was
>> and
what it was that gave it its thin light,
it was like seeing you that first morning
sitting there in the café as I picked up my spoon
to stir sugar into the cup and saw
it was woven together with strands of
your hair.

THERE ARE NO SNAKES IN IRELAND

"I can't think with an open door,"
she said, and after the door was shut
went on to say something about wind.
Wind as the source of wells.
In the beautiful vowels of a love with
no voice other than what eyes are
after tears, going down from a house called "home"
to a bridge where shock spans the violence
between suburbs and this lonely sleep. Like the
water that runs downhill to the Irish Sea
and under the thirteen bridges of Dublin,
by the breasts of Anna Livia Plurabelle
in stone. Runs like Bobbi Sands through a gap in
the hourglass of his hungry life. Runs like tears of censors
afraid of their own names. The names I had
for her, Anna Liffey, and have given you
now that the water is no longer as cold as neon,
as bright as love and light that sun shines on
in the rain and looks like you standing there on that bridge,
St. Patrick, who the pious say killed all the snakes in Ireland
even before the aftershock of ice
moved from County Cork to Kilkenny
like my lips across the tears of your poem-lost
face.
                                        Dublin, Ireland

VOICE
For Maura O'Connell

Come down from
the clouds in County Clare,
from the Burren branch
broken and daft of wind and rain
where small flowers grow in the cracks
of endless stone only a stone's throw from the sea:
this voice,
like a bell lodged in a heron's neck
that not only rings but sings,
sings swashbuckled songs that only
the *p* in pirate could steal
from the King of Hearts or
the prince of whales holding forth
a league beneath the surface of wet salt
that washes her brow with
a ring of curls in the hot lights
with high notes that go right
through the roof, go right on
singing only the best song ever sung
of scribbled then signed in blood
red as her Irish cheeks burned from wind
from the west blowing a gale that
when it comes from those lips wants
to be kissed by a major key and
maybe even a man who would be willing
to lose his mind and heart to
the quiet in a hurricane that has taken
a breath before the next verse and is working her way
back home.

MAKING LOVE IN THE LIGHTNING
WHILE LISTENING TO THUNDER IN THE RAIN

What was it
came in with
the crash of thunder
from the other side of
windows that lit up our
bodies rolling with rain?
An alibi for sleep? A reason
to weep? Or a lullaby wanting
to make love to the pain? Whatever
it was, it came. Came and kept coming
like the wind bending treetops touching
the ground, like the lost in you, found.
Foundering at the foot of the bed, breasts to
my head with hair pulled out by the root of the lack of evil
in an epiphany the size of sleet and the sweet scare
of thunder that moves inside me sliding into you as if
you weren't even there in your quicksilver hair cut like an
auroraborealis of love was only light. Light in this lightning.
In this anything but limp lust for soft skin, it might as well
be snow upagainst me that feels like heat. Feels like fingers
fused with bombs the way you touch me there that goes off like
Hiroshima and the blinding light and the bells and the sleet
against the glass groaning *is that you*? Or the two of us that
have capsized a bed in a sea of cognac that cries for a
drink we don't have but only the rain. And where rain
was there is only the drips of longing for entrails
to be intwined with you and it feels like we are and
are going down for the third time in a time of
nothing but greed now that we will
never need for anything else than this
silent swimming that feels like dreams
dreaming each other in to and out of
the air and become you forever one
with this wind blowing gentle
roses into my ear which is
there but is not in the

form of silence that
in this deafening
thunder takes
my breath
away.

NETHERWORLDS
for N.

Netherworlds are the nothing of something gone
and you are the sum of things to come.
Tell the beggar and the thief that dawn is really
all that's left of love and watch how they dance
in vain to where I already am and where
every eye in the room is on you lit up like
Saturn shows stars the way to the hub of
essence becoming silver quicker than the eye blinks and
yesterday I will come with bad mood bells on to your door
even when you're gone or giving recitals to the wind
somewhere in Wales or wonderland lit up like lasers in
your eyes.

Laugharne, Wales

NOT EVEN THE NIL OF NIGHT

Not even in the nil of night
does the doorknocking silence
seem so loud as
when she called my name
like the ghost of a blackbird from lips
only open to the kiss of air
entering my sleep so sound
that there are dreams drawing
up to the edge of morning not even
the sun could see   so far away
it is that I have spent
my life waiting for light from
the first moment I saw her there
running
away from the waves
farther and farther toward only
a line of sky leaving
only the memory of feet in the sand where
maybe somewhere she is and
is waiting   out of breath and
understands the cosmic-consciousness of morning and
the truth that
wherever she is
I am.

SAY THE UNSPOKEN WORD

Say the unspoken word
and
make me a memory
Take my name down from the marquis
Tell our mothers we don't care
and have gone off somewhere to fight
Have gone to town to sell our wings
Tired of the way love rubs wrong the music
and leaves dust
Rust of what was polished bronze before
It was buried in peat

Sing the lost chord or the last refrain of silence
and
move me to tears
Move me away from the burning fire
Tell those that have read my poems
that they were all written with stolen flames
Sunspots lifted from the mouths of saints
Babysbreath taken from the lips of burned books
Crooks climbing in windows for the Thief of Light

Think the last thought
and
remind them of reading
Tell the thinkers fond of games
we have run out of dimes
Riddled the life out of wombs
immaculate or chaste in the convent of a smile
Where I have been locked up
in rooms of wind
that blow like words do
after angry books of love unwritten
and
before I walked away.

VII.

IRIS

IRIS
     for Nan

Lips.
Lips like the fever of
forget-me-nots wanting to be iris
and not wanting to
die at the end of spring, cover my sleep.
Cover me quilt-warm even as
the loss of you lingers like shy tears
behind this mask of being in love and the lover
who is listening for the sound of his own kiss.

Why must we wait for the rain
when we are already wet?
Already like lake-water caressing the earthy sex
of the shore.

Somewhere beneath the windrow of numbers we
have mowed and raked into time,
the dew is turning to heat.
Into a flower's wings
that want us to fly!

Here! Take the *duende* in Lorca's night like
the bouquet I have made for you wrapped up in poems.
This is why we are here. Is why I have built my own bed.
A vase for the sacred purple parts of you
I want to watch as you rest. My eyes making love to
every stem, leaf, and stamen in your dreams!

MOOD SWINGS

Press you lips to my face.
Take something fleshless from my cheeks.
Call it the absence of things
or
the dreamed-of absence of fire.

Let the future of autumn know
that this act of love is really only
the death of June.
That the thought of soft cool wind
is the blood that keeps us alive.

When you go down on your knees,
even the Andes shake like a
dove shuddering its wings.
Why do you refer to this as prayer?
Is God happy with how we beg?

If you were to ask anyone now
why a poet's mood is enough to shape the sky,
all that would appear in the clouds
would be wild sex or the wish for rain.

Come, raise yourself up from
that beggar's pose.
We've come too far for
old habits and dreams of dirt.
Let's talk about tigers
and
the transfigurative aerodynamics of wings!
These things.
That like uncommon magic,
makes lava out of lightning
lying dormant in our words
and sings!

THE GARDEN

Inside these walls
there is something growing like a fireleaf
coming up from the naked body of a woman's stem.
I have come here to learn of the fire
and of the stem, and to know the heat
from her body when she does the Dance of Love.
Here, bordered by the silence in rock,
there is more food than one man can
ever eat. Leafy greens. Tubers and roots.
Flower petals. And hard-shelled grain—
A bounty for every man in love.
Sometimes after weeding the radish row I
wander over into the corn.
I have seen her there, peeping through the stalks,
out of the corner of my eye.
Yet she is never there.
Someday I will pull those old cornstalks
out from their finger-like grip on the earth
and with nowhere to hide she will watch
as she makes love to the absence of night
as the sun goes down
and she dusts off the moon with
her hair.

TRANSLATION

for Jack Gilbert

"I am leaving," she said.
It was more like code
than conversation.
More like sun-talk than
anything that might come from the moon.
Yet her face reflected in the night sun
was, for my eyes, too much light.
I just sat there
counting the letters in those three words
and I never got the same count twice.
It was either "she love me,"
or "she love me not."
Never seventeen, nineteen,
or twenty-three.
The next night as
I got ready for bed,
I heard the crickets through the window
out in the potato field
beyond the garden, counting.
After a hundred and sixty-three,
my numbers became letters.
The crickets chirping became language
that was almost song.
I translated the letters, making words,
all night long.
In the morning, there was a note
in her hand on the kitchen table.
Five words born from darkness and
the mystery of unknown codes.
"I have changed my mind."

BREAST FEEDING

It may as well have been Greece, there
that night in New York, with the rain
dripping onto her window ledge and
twilight covering the city like a golden shroud.
It was too late for dinner
even though the table was set and
the baby asleep in its bed.
The rain and the infant hunger growing
in my stomach, reminded me of childhood
in the southern mountains and how each summer
afternoon it stormed. And how calm it was
after the thunder and lightning had moved on.
After we made love and
after a long while, she said, "I ache."
The warm milk from her large breasts
tasted like Greek honey
lying there by the window looking up
at the golden rain.

WET ROADS

The road is wet and
I am the world's last black bird.
My ears are soundproof from the roar of the sea.
My eyes are lighthouses gone dim.
My feet sore from running errands for the world.
I have stolen my nose from the Sphinx
and the smell of iris evades even my deepest sleep.

Tired from the world's work,
I have come to your door
like strips of bald black tires
that lay off on the soft shoulder of the road.
A woodscolt wound down from
a whole heap of young love.

Your hands pull the lace back from
the piece of glass in the door.
Could this lace at midnight be the foreskin of my gun?
You open the door with
the white skin of your waist.
You look like water
running down for my lips.
But this is not a desert
and I'm cold.
Your eyes are a blanket
that will cover what is dry in me.
There is more than one way of being lost.
Even a wet road leads to you.

County Clare, Ireland

HOMELANDS

In the Marquesas, the villagers brought the
breadfruit and chickens down the mountain to the rafts.
For more than a month the sailors
stayed afloat as an act of faith,
looking for land. For Hava Iki
which they called "home."
Like those ancient travelers,
I set out on the raft of your body
sailing and drifting to find
a port-of-call.
Among the peaks of intense sacredness,
the silverswords stand out like the fingers
of my hands that have colonized your skin.
Have painted your lips the color of mirrors.
Have entered you
as the sky is pierced by a man in the moon each night.
After a thousand years, I am still digging
in the sand for clams. After a thousand more
only the middens will be left as a memory of food.
It is late at night
and in the moonlight I whisper your name.
"Weyeepi," I moan in the half light.
Either you are sleeping or
have left. Gone off on the rafts
of sailors and ghosts.
This is your land, and I am just
a white intruder here. An herbivore
in a land of meat, feeding on love.
How could the gods of emptiness even think
of letting you go?
Like a new native, I will be here forever.
A thousand miles from where I was born
and, like you, calling it "home."

WRITING

In the woods of heaven
every man in love with ink is
trying to escape.
Yet, no man runs.
Only looks out through trees into meadows
beyond limbs of greening leaves, hoping
for the form of a woman's body
in a wish of stars.

A POEM FOR A MAN MARRIED IN MOUNTAINS
for Nan

This is a poem written by a man married
in mountains, to mountains, by a mountain stream.

This is a song written by a man married to music,
married to the sound of wind in a fence
with perfect pitch and key.

This is psalm written by a man
married to the woman of white hair
with a smile of red roses.

This is a prayer uttered by a man married
to the Watkins of a Welshwoman
in a castle in Wales.

This is a book of changes penned by a man married
on a *ben* or bald to a game of chance.

This is a palindrome written by a man married
to the woman of red roses under a sea-blue sky
in the wind.

This is a thesis written by a man married
to the queen of hearts in a thistle
in a field of peat.

This is a mirror made by a man married
to the reflection of rhyme, to time
in a face.

This is a mask molded by a man married
with a ring of coal for her fingers
and a ring of bronze for her feet.

This is a spell of majik cast by a man married
on moss, with ferns like flags flying
in a *wee glen*.

This is a garden planted by a man married
to the *kelt* of yellow iris and the dream of earth
seeking sleep.

This is a poem written by a man married
with a heart of blackbirds
to a woman with the heart of crows.

This is a liturgy written by a man married
by the god in a *moor* with more heather and gorse
than a priest.

This is a dressing doctored by a man married
to the dream of health, with elixir alive
in his blood.

This is a sacrament shared by a man married
to the maiden hair of fern and the love of a twin
twined as one in this way.
Both.
On the mountain.
Today.

Glenfinnan Gorge, Scotland
1995

FIRSTS

It starts with something silver.
Like a moon's halo surrounding the lips.
Just beyond a hint of sun in her eyes.
This is how it begins. With the silver
rushing like a river down her shoulders
and back. Running.
Running water that by the time
it reaches her waist it will be
time for both of us to die.
To begin breathing beyond what is
only breath as she takes mine away
by only walking into a room that
is full of beautiful people and
only half her age.
If I were to draw a line
with my eyes from her waist
to the bottoms of her feet,
it would be drawn in hair.
And to know the distance
of that line would be the
sum of geometry and the wind
giving spring to those mortal coils.
Coils against cheeks so milk white
that even the antlers of elk to my
touch wouldn't be rubbing velvet.
Milk that my lips drink from
high bones on her face or
her breasts even before we make love
for the first time in water where
the womb of our love began.
Began in her silver hair.
In a room. With chests beating
like the frap and flutter from the wings of small birds
against the clear fall air.
Where we were virgin to this tradition,
to this tithe of hearts
given, and like the water, beyond thirst.

THIS INK IS THE EARTH

*"Something has been let loose in rain;
it is teaching us to love."*
-Joy Harjo

This ink is the earth.
Brown wet water.
Dark as your skin that even the night
won't take away like a thief
looking for jewels.

This earth I stand on
is in the ink.
The run-off of melted bones.
The after-shock
of all our collected dreams—
These words are how the
ink and the earth make love.

I am the earth.

You are the water.

I am the paper.

You are the ink.

And if you are a red horse
then I am a black bird. A dark moon
camouflaged behind the lashes in trees.

Meanwhile, the a b c's of seriousness have
stolen the blues. Have read, writ, and arithmetic'd
the blush right out of my smile. Brainwashed the earth
from giving up clay.
What can I say?
That it's ok or that ss shouldn't rhyme?
You're all mine.
Wherever there are plowed fields of shadow moving in dreams
and your eyes are my memory of ink.

LEI
> *for Nan*

In a land of flowers
our theme for the week was
"a lei a day."
and so each morning
I presented her with garlands of orchids,
halos of plumeria,
and ropes of ti.
And each night,
she gave me the best rose
of her fragrant sex.

If this had gone on for long,
the islands would have been reduced to
nothing more than their history of
volcanic rock.
Our bodies
wilted garlands withered and pale.
Yet, what joy we brought
 to each other's necks
and at night to our bed
with a crashing surf outside
and in the morning a chorale
of thousands of small blue birds.

Friends laugh when we tell them
of our week in paradise
and the adage of "a lei a day."
They think it
some Hawaiian humor
we brought home in our kitsch-filled bags.
Ah, but the joke is on them,
as you can see it in our smiles
still   at bedtime in our old age.
Memories, like colored tides of climax,
that cover us in petal waves.
The refuge of our place in dreams.

Kona, Hawaii/ 1999

THE LIE THAT LIVES

Moments are only small eternities covered
In the silent centuries of your grace.
Canons going off in the gunneries of
Another autumn day like a memory medicine men have conjured
    with love.

January has gone on long enough and
Eternity is weeping at night with
All the pain that distance brings when you're gone, and
Nothing will change the death of this little lie that
    is you in me,
      that lives!

THE WILD DUCKS AT COOLE
for Nan

Where the wild ducks at Coole
Wade and quack in the river for a
Grab of green grass growing
Near the brown rocks
Covered with moss and the
History of walls is
Where we have come to
Honor trees
By carving our names with knives
In gardens for those who come from Ballylee
And towers where swords of samurai float in
The air of rooms ruined by love
And through woods and on paths
For walking where we,
Like howling horsemen, pass by and
Are here to see swans
That are only here in autumn
Wild as these ducks or
How I see you   non-ethnic but
As white as the wind in your hair.

Coole Park
County Galway, Ireland
1995

THE ALMAMATER OF A KISS
For C.L.

Only the alma mater of space will wait for
what's going down in the deltas of human life and
the inlets of what was once Mars and now is
the bar-room brawl of belief that smothers our
dreams dreaming of what the sex of salvation is
about to become any instant as the orbiting aura
of Earth is turning black in the absence of light
which I see in your eyes eyeless and almost
like rain would be if I were apples and
needed to grow, go, gorge myself on the photo-
synthesis of your skin seeking itself in what's
left of me or to the right of politics reaching
into the cookie-jar of your soul for sugar and
pulling out instead   my kiss.

IMMORTALITY

When I write on your white skin with
dark ink and the calligraphy of unspoken vowels
covers arms and legs   page-like,
covers back, belly and thighs
and the thought that is born from words
makes midnight blink and the morning go blind,
I find the wherewithal to
make my mistakes   indelible
and
stained in truth so that
they will last   even after
your body has gone to the morgue
and only ashes remain
on stretched canvas
as a work of art.

WHERE THE WHITE WAVES

Where the white waves
wear away the sand and
land is where I rest my feet
swaggering along the warm and
quiet shore   talking to gulls
and pelican pulling the
aereodite air along in the
beak-biffing foam of waves wherever
no man is or fish are
in eyes so old that not even the
aurora borealis of sound could hear
the sea-squawking song now
not even coming from all that noise
not counting the million
grains of sand in one square inch
of a happy thought there
inside the dark of a crab hole
I look in to wonder what
is there amongst the lack of
sea oats and
find only you.

THE BLUE ROSE OF VENICE
for Nan

Too much time has gone by
since I have put my love for her
into actions or in words.
To make up for
my manly lack of romance,
I buy tickets to Venice
with money I don't have.
In a city where voices
sound more like music than human talk,
we wander the streets and canals
on our first night.
Someone is selling roses for a Euro
near the Bridge of Sighs.
With the strange silver coin in my pocket,
I choose the only one in the bunch
that is blue
(to match her linen dress
and her hair in the light of the moon)
which I place in a wine bottle
in the window
of our convent room.
In the morning,
the sound of skylarks
is what we hear.
In Titian's light,
a poem of indigo
against red rooftops
is what we see.

DANCING IN THE PIAZZA SAN MARCO

First night in Venice.
we sit with pigeons
and crescent moon
drinking wine
in the Piazza San Marco.

At midnight
the B-flat bells of the campanile
fill our ears
and the big piazza.
Nearby, a small symphonic band
plays "Moon River" then
"Al Di La."
Rising from my seat,
I reach for her hand.
We walk to the center
of this huge open space
lit by large electric candles and the moon.
Embracing,
we dance
to a Venetian waltz,
in slow circles,
round and round the square.

LAST LOVE POEM

Down to my last word or crumb
of the food of love I feed on
like the water it takes to make rice I
weep watering a last page of vowels
ripe for your heart and the hope
that your thirst for sunlight will
want to watch it grow!

ACKNOWLEGEMENTS

The author wishes to acknowledge the editors of the following periodicals, books and anthologies in which many of the poems in this collection first appeared: *Beatitude, Art Matters, BullHead, Nexus, N.C. Poetry Society Award Winning Poems, Western Slopes Connections, The Asheville Poetry Review, Invisible Academy, Sun, Waters, Paper Air, Katuah, Southern ARC, Heartland, the Arts Journal, Wayah Review, Anthology of Magazine Verse, Yearbook of American Poetry (1988), Blue Ridge Parkway 50th Anniversary Anthology, Atlanta Review, Aldrava (Brazil), Milestone, Lacrosse (France), Northwords (Scotland), The Cuirt Journal (Ireland), Poetry Ireland Review (Ireland), Litterature en Marche (France), 5AM.*

"Learning To Dance" and "What Is Woven" were first published as letterset limited editions broadsheets by Landlocked Press (Tatlin Books) in Madison, Wisconsin in 1986.

"The Garden" was first published by Holocene Press as a limited edition broadside in 1993.

"Mirrors of the Moon" was first published in conjunction with a collaborative public poetry and dance performance at the Dance America Festival in Chicago in 1992--where it was a finalist and winner of the College Dance & Performance Competition.

"Blue Rose of Venice" and "Dancing in the Piazza San Marco" first appeared in the Limited Edition collection <u>The Blue Rose of Venice</u> *published by Mountains &Rivers Press in 2009.*

ABOUT THE AUTHOR

Thomas Rain Crowe is a prize-winning poet and an internationally-published author of thirty books, including the multi-award winning book of nonfiction *Zoro's Field: My Life in the Appalachian Woods (2005)*; *The Laugharne Poems(* 1997); and the Celtic language anthology *Writing the Wind: A Celtic Resurgence*. As an editor, he has worked with *Beatitude* magazine, *Katuah Journal* and the *Asheville Poetry Review*. He is founder and publisher of New Native Press. He lives in rural western North Carolina.

author photo by Kenn Long